BUTTERFLIES

PowerKiDS press.

New York

Suzanne Slade

To my grandmother, Marguerite Buckingham (aka "Cookie Grandma")

Published in 2008 by The Rosen Publishing Group, Inc.
29 East 21st Street, New York, NY 10010

First Edition

Editor: Joanne Randolph
Book Design: Julio Gil
Photo Researcher: Nicole Pristash

Photo Credits: Cover, pp. 1, 5, 7, 9, 11, 13, 15, 21 © Shutterstock.com; pp. 11 (inset), 17 © Dennis Kunkel Microscopy, Inc.; p. 19 © istockphoto.com/Jill Lang.

Library of Congress Cataloging-in-Publication Data

Slade, Suzanne.
  Butterflies / Suzanne Slade. — 1st ed.
      p. cm. — (Under the microscope: backyard bugs)
  Includes index.
  ISBN-13: 978-1-4042-3821-3 (library binding)
  ISBN-10: 1-4042-3821-2 (library binding)
  1. Butterflies—Juvenile literature. I. Title.
  QL544.2.S53 2008
  595.78'9—dc22
                                      2007005567

Manufactured in the United States of America

Contents

Beauty in Your Backyard

On a warm summer day, you may see colorful winged **insects** called butterflies floating in your backyard. Butterflies like to live in **habitats** that are filled with plants and flowers. They are often found in open fields with wildflowers or near a backyard flower garden.

As they fly, butterflies move up and down. Butterflies search for flowers where they can get a sweet snack. They might stop on a bush or tree to rest. A butterfly may even land on you! Flying or resting, colorful butterflies are beautiful visitors in your backyard.

If a butterfly lands on you, be careful not to hurt your colorful neighbor. It will soon move on to find a sweet-tasting flower.

Flying Friends

Butterflies are an important part of your backyard habitat. They provide food for birds and animals. Butterflies also help make new flowers by spreading **pollen** when they stop for a drink.

There are many flying insects with large, colorful wings in your backyard, but not all these are butterflies. Butterflies have flying friends that look like them, called moths. By learning a few simple clues, you can easily spot a true butterfly. Most moths are light brown or white, while butterflies are brightly colored. Moths often fly at night. Butterflies take flight during the day.

These are butterflies. A moth generally has a hairier body than a butterfly does, and it is not as brightly colored.

Butterflies Around the World

About 18,000 species, or different kinds, of butterflies live all around the world. People are still discovering new species today. Even as new species are being found, though, some types of butterflies may become **extinct**. New buildings, roads, and farms crowd butterflies out of their homes. Sprays that people use to kill harmful insects are also a danger to butterflies.

Monarchs and swallowtails are common butterflies in North America. The monarch's wings have orange and black stripes and white spots around the edges. A tiger swallowtail butterfly has large, yellow wings with black stripes. Each wing has a long, thin tail.

There are many different kinds of swallowtail butterflies, each with different colors and markings on their wings. This is a tiger swallowtail.

Colorful Wings

One of the first things you will notice on a butterfly is its colorful wings. Its four wings are covered with thin, flat pieces, called scales. Thousands of tiny colored scales make beautiful marks on a butterfly wing. These scales rub off easily. Some fall off when a butterfly beats its wings.

A butterfly's wings are on the middle part of its body, called the thorax. Its six legs are found on the bottom of the thorax. A butterfly's tiny head has two **compound eyes**, for spotting flowers and enemies. On top of the head are two long **antennae**, which help the butterfly smell and feel.

This labeled picture of a butterfly shows all the body parts. *Inset:* This close-up shot of the butterfly's wing scales shows how the scales overlap like roof tiles do.

10

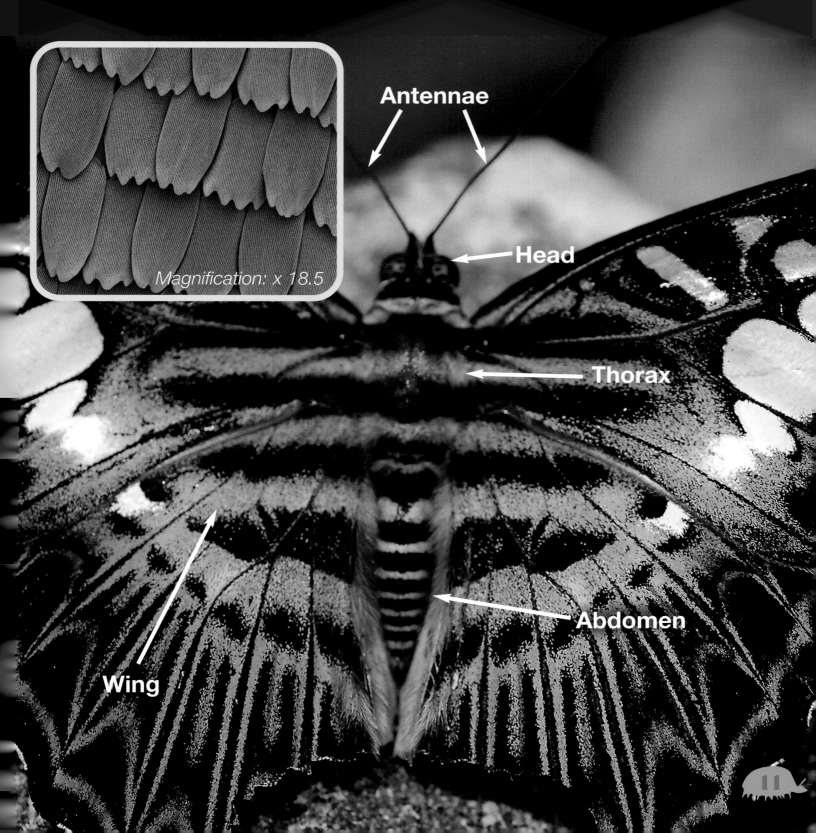

Antennae

Head

Thorax

Abdomen

Wing

Magnification: x 18.5

11

A Butterfly's Life

Most butterflies lay their eggs in the warmth of spring or summer. These eggs **hatch** two to three weeks after they are laid. Butterfly eggs turn dark just before small worms, called caterpillars, squirm out. Caterpillars spend most of their time eating plants. As they grow, caterpillars **shed** their old, tight skin.

After shedding four or five times, a caterpillar glues itself to a branch. Then it sheds one last time and becomes a pupa. The hard shell on the outside of a pupa is called a chrysalis. After a few days or months, the pupa changes into a butterfly.

This pupa hangs from a branch, while a new butterfly waits to come out of the case.

Making New Butterflies

To make a butterfly egg, a **male** and **female** butterfly must become a pair and **mate**. Butterflies find each other by sight and smell. They use their compound eyes to look for butterflies with certain colors and marks on their wings. They also use their antennae to find a butterfly with the right smell. Males and females both give off a special smell that gets the other's attention.

Once a male and female find each other and mate, the female butterfly flies off to lay her eggs. Most butterflies lay their eggs on a plant that the caterpillars can eat once they hatch.

Much of a butterfly, from its wings to its head, is built to help it find a mate. A butterfly uses its eyes and antennae to find a mate with the right colors and smell.

14

Favorite Foods

Most butterflies drink nectar, a sweet juice that flowers make. Butterflies see flowers with their eyes and smell them with their antennae. Once a butterfly lands on a flower, it unrolls a long strawlike tongue on its head to drink. Some kinds of butterflies chew on plants with their strong mouth. A butterfly stores and breaks down food in its **abdomen**.

Caterpillars are very picky eaters. Most will eat only one kind of plant. Female butterflies are careful to lay their eggs on the type of plant they know their young will eat.

This is a magnified, or much larger, look at a butterfly's tongue, called a proboscis or galea. When the butterfly is not eating, the tongue is curled up against its head.

Magnification: x 18

17

Watch Out, Butterfly!

Butterflies have many **predators**. Lizards, frogs, spiders, and some large bugs enjoy a tasty butterfly meal. Birds are a butterfly's number-one enemy. With their sharp eyes and fast wings, they can easily catch a butterfly while it is resting or flying.

Butterflies have many ways to keep safe. Some butterflies hide using **camouflage**. They pull their wings closed so they stand up over their back. The bottom of their wings can look like part of a plant. Other butterflies scare their enemies with eyespots, round spots on their wings that look like animal eyes.

This lizard has made a tasty snack out of this butterfly. Butterflies have ways to keep themselves safe, but sometimes they don't work!

When the Cold Wind Blows

Butterflies are cold-blooded animals. Their body does not make heat, so they need to live in warm places. Many species fly south in winter. This flight is called migration. Some butterflies, such as the monarch, will fly up to 2,000 miles (3,219 km) on a migration trip. Once butterflies arrive at a new, warm home, they gather in large groups and sleep.

Some butterflies stay where they are and hibernate, or sleep, during winter. When the weather turns cold in fall, they find a safe place out of the wind to sleep. Hibernating butterflies wake when spring arrives.

Here a group of butterflies has landed on some flowers. These butterflies may travel a long way before they find a winter resting place.

Enjoying Butterflies

Many kinds of butterflies will visit your backyard if you make a butterfly garden. Butterflies are known to like yellow, orange, red, and purple flowers. You can learn which plants certain butterflies eat and put those in your garden, too. For example, swallowtail butterflies like a green plant called parsley.

Add a butterfly house. Butterflies can stay in it when the weather gets bad. Butterfly houses have thin, tall doors, which allow butterflies in but keep enemies out. To remember your special visitors, take a picture or make a drawing of them.

Glossary

abdomen (AB-duh-mun) The large, back part of an insect's body.

antennae (an-TEH-nee) Thin, rodlike feelers located on the head of certain animals.

camouflage (KA-muh-flahj) A color or shape that matches what is around something and helps hide it.

compound eyes (KOM-pownd EYZ) The larger eyes of bugs, which are made up of many simple eyes.

extinct (ek-STINKT) No longer existing.

female (FEE-mayl) Having to do with women and girls.

habitats (HA-beh-tats) The kinds of land where an animal or a plant naturally lives.

hatch (HACH) To come out of an egg.

insects (IN-sekts) Small animals that often have six legs and wings.

male (MAYL) Having to do with men and boys.

mate (MAYT) To come together to make babies.

pollen (PAH-lin) A yellow dust made by the male parts of flowers.

predators (PREH-duh-terz) Animals that kill other animals for food.

shed (SHED) To get rid of an outside covering, like skin.

23

Index

A
abdomen, 16
antennae, 10, 14, 16

B
birds, 6, 18
bush, 4

C
caterpillar(s), 12, 14, 16
compound eyes, 10, 14

E
egg(s), 12, 14, 16

F
flowers, 4, 6, 16, 22
food, 6, 16

G
garden, 4, 22

H
habitat(s), 4, 6

I
insects, 4, 6, 8

M
moths, 6

P
plant(s), 4, 14, 16, 18, 22
pollen, 6
predators, 18

S
species, 8, 20

T
thorax, 10
tree, 4

W
wings, 6, 8, 10, 14, 18

Web Sites

Due to the changing nature of Internet links, PowerKids Press has developed an online list of Web sites related to the subject of this book. This site is updated regularly. Please use this link to access the list:
www.powerkidslinks.com/umbb/bfly/